Prison Segmentation For Overnight Visitors

24 Hours of Normal Family Time

Reverend Mike Wanner

Table Of Contents

Introduction

Keeping people in prisons is very costly we all need some relief from extreme taxation that results from imprisoning vast numbers of our fellow citizens. Somehow, we seem to have taken for granted that we can afford these prices.

Alas and unfortunately, the cost of incarceration is about to eat up the quality of the American Dream. We are all gradually being banished to involuntary servitude to our insecurities.

I invite the whole community to consider the situations of the incarcerated in order to see if there are fundamental, legal, appropriate, non-technical very humane ideas that can be embraced that add a perspective that may contain common sense approaches to effect change that can create possibilities for prisoners to earn the opportunity to generate taxpayer savings.

In recent times there seems to be an emphasis on eliminating prisoner visitations and restricting communications. This type of change is less humane and increased isolation may be less than productive, and there may be a possibility for multiple complications.

1 - Background

I want to trigger mindset shifts in the prisoners as well as employees and the community. We need a lot more Objective Productive Dialogues about Enhancing the lives of Prison Employees, Prisoners, Taxpayers and the Families of Each of these groups.

I hope that this book continues the work started by my other books and continues to enhance the lives of Prison Employees, Prisoners, Taxpayers and the Families of Each of these groups?

As I have been writing my early books on the subject of Prisons, the complexity of the process has been amazing to me.

I have previously published 44 books so far about the prison situations, and they fall into the following categories:

4 *Angel Raphael Speaks Books about Prisons*
1 *Prison Jobs book*
1 *Contained Care Communities: Concept*
1 *Australia In Miniature*
5 *Prison Possibilities Dialogue Series Books*
5 *Prison Possibilities Idea Books*
1 *Prison Genius Pool: "So Much Genius In Jail."*
2 *Prisoner Family Books*
9 *Prisoner Projects (Writing, Cell Clearing, and Blessings, Prisoner Professors, Prison Reiki?, Dowsing, Solitary Community, Communications, Motivation, Real Estate)*
1 *Judges and An Angel Rule On Possibilities*
1 *Ideas For Prison Wardens*
13 *Prison Segmentation Books*

2 - Why I am Writing This Book

In the process of writing the books referenced about, prisoner motivation and optimism seem very pertinent to the success of those who will someday re-enter the community.

I have previously written some books about communication and family dynamics, and I still feel they are essential to the human psyche and the rehabilitation of those who have been incarcerated.

Visitation is quite a hassle for prisoners and their families and the system. There is a lot of heartbreak around visitation because there seems to be a lot of preparatory work and financial and emotional expense around it.

Many times problems can lead to opportunities, and that can lead to efficiency and abundance of what was desired at the outset.

Let us consider here benefits for the prisoners, the families, the system and the taxpayers. Can we create a little usual family time?

3 - The Segmentation Effect

Segmentation takes incarceration to a controlled condition of freedom from the intensity of disharmonic interference that naturally flows from the congestion of too many people in too little space. The controlled separation allows possibilities for peace, tranquility, and potential for positive outcomes.

Part of the beauty of segmentation can be the ability to mitigate further personal deterioration of prisoners and allow enough pause to provide a regrouping opportunity for each participant.

The treasure for each participant could be the opportunity to be safe for a while from specific stressors that are not compatible with peace of mind and or personal safety.

An individual's ability to apply for a pause from the intensity of everybody else's stress can go a long way to keep the peace and harmony of a facility. The judgment of a sentence may be too much for some people to process and may take them closer to the dark side of their being than they would usually go

The idea that there could be options to experiences that disturb them could allow many people to have hopes that would not otherwise exist.

People are fragile, and there is little value in missing no-cost opportunities that might prevent episodes of upheaval. Personal peace in Prison can promote community tranquility and freedom from pushback.

4 - Slow Down and Enjoy

In the past, the goal for visitation seemed to be to have some time together and serve as many people as possible. That must not be very efficient because it seems there is a lot of movement away from that process.

Resources seem to be minimal in prison, so this proposal is about optimizing the resources available and trying to deliver a longer more valuable, more beneficial experience that can make a positive impact on each person visited and their visitors.

There have been many segmentations ideas suggested, and hopefully, facilities will be able to create ones that serve their residents well. When a prisoner has benefitted enough to stabilize their interests and plans, it may be time to start working towards some overnight visits so that family reconnection can be optimal.

We will need to discuss the practical side of the issue first. We need to define a location process and plan that will eliminate all preparation hassles and plan the quality of the time that prisoners and family members spend together.

When one prisoner has a small time block with one or more family members, there may be little time to have quality time with anybody.

Being present and having a personal connection may be entirely different things.

5 - Efficiency and Connectivity

Little Time can equal a very little connection which could be a loss of opportunity at a cost to the facility which may not be worth the effort or help to keep the bond that existed before incarceration.

Out of Sight - Out of Mind

People's connections can exist in a fluid state, and sometimes voids are filled with choices that can develop into very permanent participations that are different than the one preferred.

Child development may be an excellent example of replacement participation. Children are growing in their awareness of all things and as they become the experience or lack thereof can leave a reminder that stays for a longer time.

Spouses also have needs for human interaction may be an excellent example of replacement participation. Social connection is part of life, and the support experience or lack thereof in the life living process can leave a reminder that stays for a long time.

Memory fades over time, and the bonds that hold a family or a relationship together can weaken as memory fades. A substantial length of visits could contribute to the security of family relationships and strengthen the foundation of each family so that support for reentry is optimized. Visits shortly before reentry could break the ice of transition so the whole family can blend smoothly.

6 - Each Person Needs Time to Adjust

A brief meeting with one or many family members may not be enough to smooth the reentry for a prisoner.

The logic behind a lot more time for prisoners to reconnect with individuals is an idea that can serve well the whole family before they are living together 24 hours a day and seven days a week.

If you buy new shoes and wear them all day right after the purchase, you may have no discomfort. Sometimes people who do that can have trouble and cause irritation that brings pain and or the need to go back and wait for that to heal.

The idea with shoes and people is to ease into situations, so there is no stress and no complications of importance. There has been a saying that "You do not know people until you live with them (anon.)."

Some might say that you do know them from before they were incarcerated. While that may be true, there exists the possibility that the person is no longer the same as before they were imprisoned.

Spouses and children may also be different people over time, and it would be helpful if all personalities could be reintroduced gradually, so there are no clashes triggered by changes that were not expected. Preparation can help to ensure the success of reentry into the community.

7 - Each Person Needs Comfort

The meeting of prisoners with different members of their family may be crucial to the success of their reentry. Getting a good start can be important in many things and reentry could be high on that list.

In Walt Disney's "Mary Poppins", there was a song about struggle, and it declared how a slight reframing of a challenge could be helpful in being able to cope with things that are viewed as distasteful. The song was about using just a little bit of sugar to help the medicine go down.

Remember the jingle as you read the words;

"A Spoonful of sugar helps the medicine go down
The medicine go down.
The medicine go down
Just a spoonful of sugar helps the medicine go down
In a most delightful way."

Family time can help comfort a prisoner and family members in transition like a spoonful of sugar can help get the medicine down "…in a most delightful way."

Disney media can help many people in many ways as they focus on the transportation of Joy to us all. Disney messages can be beneficial. This is not a commercial, but I hope it reminds you of the kind of tools that can help bring everybody peace. When words are difficult to find, watching Disney may have a treasure chest of shared experience.

8 - Children Are Innocent

Children of prisoners are innocent of crime but may feel penalized by the school system, community systems, and the prison system as they may be at a loss for the support that they need from their Family. The number of children may be in the millions.

We may have as many as two million children who are actively impacted by the complications of their parents being in lockup. Children could be very influential in the healing of their parents if they had the opportunity to talk with them.

Children may be significantly traumatized by other children for being unsupported by parents at events and in general. Children can be cruel, and the trauma of name-calling can last a long time.

There are many things said about children of prisoners that can be disturbing to children, parents and teachers and some of the pain can be long-lasting. Please think about some of them:

1. Is it true that the children will be better off if they have no contact with incarcerated parents?

2. Are children with incarcerated parents described as badly parented?

3. Is it true that children with incarcerated parents are poorly parented?

4. Should states decline visitation or another regular contact between prisoners and their children?

5. Are prisoners at a detriment by not having contact with their children?

6. Do prisoners benefit from maintaining contact with their children and how much?

7. Do children benefit from maintaining contact with their prisoner-parent and how much?

8. If parents are not able to visit their children, are they exempt from abandonment challenges?

9. Do children have a legal right to maintain a relationship with an incarcerated parent?

10. Do children have a legal right to terminate their parent's rights to parental custody?

11. Does any government agency have the charge to look out after the needs of children of the incarcerated?

So many variables can make it hard for children of the incarcerated, but that does not mean that the children would not want to see their parent/s.

9 - Children Have Healing Energy

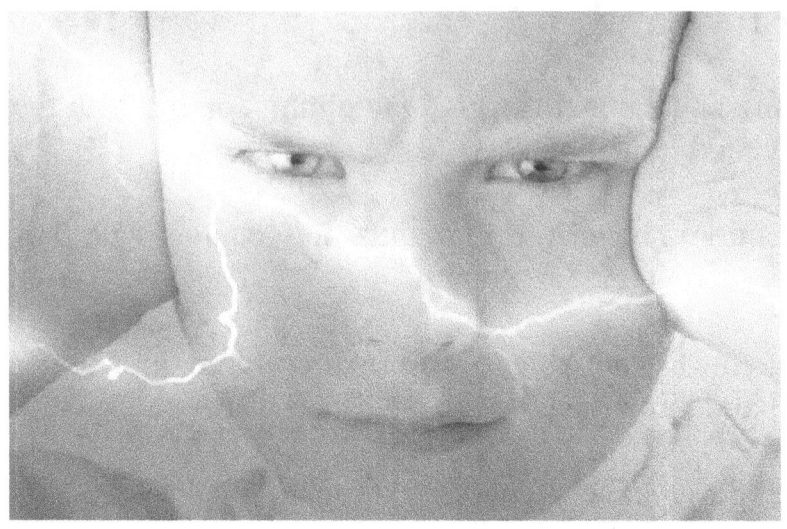

Children have healing energy, and I wrote a book about the title of this chapter with that same name. The emphasis of that book was about showing the children pictures and how to deal with people and how to act.

The invitation for the children who read that book was one of behaving in a safe environment so that one is well received and maintains their status in a group.

Unfortunately, some children of prisoners may not feel that kind of safety because the support is lacking through no fault of their own. Isolation from parent/s may be traumatizing and could supersede other priorities.

Children may have a tendency to blame themselves when situations have changed for the worse. Absent evidence to the contrary from authorities like parents, teacher, and others, children can carry guilt for things that are not their responsibility.

An overnight visit with a parent could bring a real level of normalcy and safety which might be significant to keep a child on a path or striving for better days.

10 - Dad Could Share In the Healing Energy

Children bring out the best in all of us. Dads and Moms can catch motivation from their children as they give them the love that the children need so much.

Giving and receiving can easily be reciprocated in a little bit of regular family time. One can easily get lost in possibilities when there is the right motivation for them.

Family can harmonize with other members at a level of balance that can bring fantastic energy to the interchange. That harmony can incline all participants to move their personal power into a relaxed state that is called homeostasis where healing happens.

Prison can interact with a person like a dead electrical outlet can communicate with a cell phone. When there is no energy flowing, the charge depletes, and the cell phone is useless.

People in prison can be empty of energy or depleted so much that they do not function as an optimized human being.

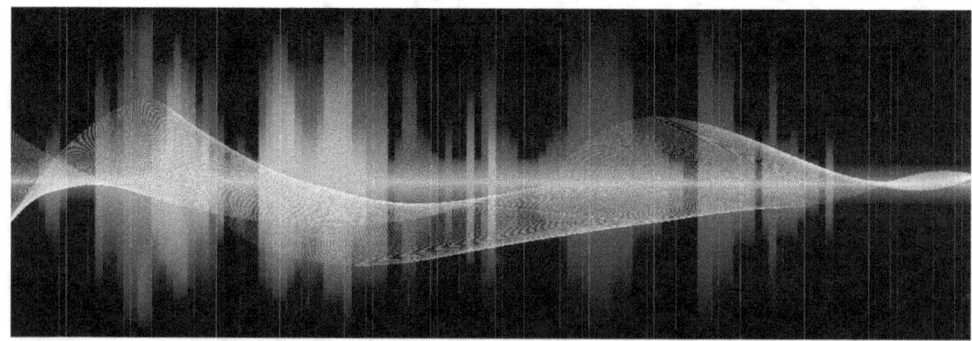

11 - Prisoner's Family Needs to Interact

Two Heads Are Better Than One

Jail can be very lonely for one spouse and at home without their spouse can be very lonely for the other. Time to talk can smooth relationships.

Whether a couple is alone or has children, there are extended family dynamics about everything that needs to be discussed. The easier it is to deal with it all, the more likely that the details will be handled in a way that is not disruptive to the relationship.

The Extended Family Dynamics

The dynamics in extended families continue when people are in prison, and the free family members can lose sight of the limitations for the one in jail, The family member at home can get a lot of pressure, and perhaps some of that will be helpful and some not.

The more explicit that couples are with extended families, the better off for all concerned. The important thing may be to say no, or I don't know and keep yourself from hard feelings as much as possible.

12 - Family Together Time

Togetherness Is Simply Awesome For Each Family Member.
What You Do Together Is Insignificant.
Unity is The Bliss.

13 - Why Overnight

Families have a regular pattern of spending time together in the same house overnight. Elongated visits can help with the dynamics of bonding or re-bonding to reestablish the bonds that once were.

Cuddling can be soothing to everyone in the family and allow a relaxation period that is stress-free or at least stress reductive. When stress can dissipate, it becomes easier to bring up sensitive issues in a way that they can be examined and decided upon.

Overnight also can make sense for the host facility as they can Get a lot of value (family time together) with only one process of check-in. The added cost is zero. The benefit to the host facility is priceless and peaceful.

Cuddle Up

Stress Down

Peacefulness Up

Violent Tendencies Down

Personally Safe Time Period

Prisoner Sanity Time

Peace In The Valley All Night Long

Old Issue Mediation

Families may have patterns of old issues that need to be settled that cannot resolve themselves when the family is split up. Bringing the family back together overnight is a healing opportunity to find new balance and understanding. Remedial balance can begin a new vibrancy to the family.

Family Business Dynamics

Families have needs and working together can get people back on the same page. Children grow and have a need to share their views on everything with parents so that guidance can flow.

Improved readiness for scholastic accomplishments alone could be life-changing for the children.

A Little Cuddle Goes a Long Way

Cuddle Time - Tuning Fork Effect

When families harmonize with each other, they have an impact on the quality of each other's life.

14 - Visitation Space Justification

Space for visitation will need to be justified before a plan can be approved. As a big believer in participation, I would invite facilities to share this writing with selective residents and encourage feedback.

To incentivize productive feedback, let me propose some ideas for potential contributors to consider:

1. Committee participation will not give you an exclusive right for involvement so if you do not come with the intention of the highest good for the greater community; then you might be well advised to step back.

2. This is not going to happen just because the proverbial "they" should give you some benefits.

3. The way to create such potential would be behavior that is very patient, selfless and community oriented.

4. The rules must be developed in a careful manner.

5. Contributors to the success need encouragement.

6. It would be wise to network with resource providers.

7. It would be wise to network for resources.

15 - Visitation Space Layout & Support

Space for visitation will need to be created from what already exists that can be repurposed. Please think as if you are building a benefit for many people that can begin to change perceptions and possibilities.

Each prison will have a different layout so your realignment of space could be entirely different than anybody else that you hear about. One step at a time is the way to go so that success is embraced as early on as possible.

Each successful effort can be instrumental in the creation of another try. The most important part could be the completion of the first attempt.

It may be helpful also to ask participants if this type of visitation could offer their visitors some cost savings that might be enough for them to kick in some of their savings to a little cash fund that could help to enhance the experience for visitors.

Visitors could be informed that contributions to the startup costs could be instrumental in the ability to making it happen. Ongoing support could be helpful but would not be as critical as the first effort to change the possibilities for future hospitality.

16 - Prison Benefits

Each prison could make some effort to create the ability to host some elongated visits on a progressive basis to continue the potential. An ideal way to do that might be to have the extra work be rewarded financially for the prison.

I am not proposing here that we turn this into a business but that we try to create a bit of subsidy for the consideration of doing this by the facility. The idea would be to pay back the expense of hosting the program.

Of course, the reimbursement might lead to claims of preferential treatment, but that can be avoided by making the payments optional and secret. Visitation rules set the stage for success.

Records of successful reentries could go a long way toward changing the image and the possibilities of prisons. Citizens and taxpayers could soon see that imprisonment done right can have a benefit to the quality of life for everybody forevermore.

Families staying and growing together on a progressive basis can reduce recidivism and improve facility safety.

Future Discussions

Many prisons may have issues with conjugal visits on a variety of basis. There are many cultural, religious, social, and practical reasons that may incline authorities to lean one way or the other. A future discussion could help understanding.

For

Considering

These

Ideas

Ever

It Does Not Help Prayer Still Does!

Resource: http://Create-A-Prayer.com

19 - Resource List

Distant Healing Sessions (or Join Mail List) – Write To
mikewann@voicenet.com

Books by Rev. Mike at www.Amazon.com:

Veterans Healing Six Pack
1. *Trauma Healing Options for VA Hospitals: Help for Veterans to Own Their Healing and their future.*
2. *Trauma Healing Action Steps for Veterans: Help to Start Healing*
3. *Trauma Healing Action Steps for Veterans: Empowerment*
4. *Trauma Healing Action Steps for Veterans: Forgiveness*
5. *Trauma Healing Action Steps for Veterans: Thought Freedom*
6. *Tea For Veterans: Welcome One Home*

PTSD Power Pack:
1. *The PTSD Project: Turn Pain To Power*
2. *PTSD & Soul Retrieval: Putting One Back Together*
3. *PTSD & The Purple PAD: Calling all Scientists and PTSD Patients*

Angel Raphael Speaks Volume 1: Take Courage! God Has Healing in Store for You!
Angel Raphael Speaks Volume 2: Take Courage! God Has Healing in Store for You!
Angel Raphael Speaks Volume 3: Take Courage! God Has Healing in Store for You!
Angel Raphael Speaks Volume 4: Angels, Addicts, Alcoholics & Prisoners – Oh Yeah!
Angel Raphael Speaks Volume 5: Prisoners Caring for Alcoholics - Australia In Miniature Projects Intro
Angel Raphael Speaks Volume 6: Prisoners Caring for Addicts - Australia In Miniature For Addicts
Reiki Journaling from Japan
Reiki Is Alive: God's Great Gift
Four Parts to Healing
Distant Healing: We Are All Connected

Prison Reiki? Maybe Someday? A Gateway To Help Heal Prisons &
   America?
Judges and An Angel Rule On Possibilities: We Can Cut Sentences &
Prison Costs
Ideas For Prison Wardens: Leadership Is Not Easy
Solitary Community: Could Community Support Cut Costs and Issues?
Prison Project Communications Team: Communications Can Change
Lives
Motivating & Empowering Prisoners? Invite Prisoners To Find Their
Motivation
Prison Segmentation For Safety, And Sanity, Security, Peace, and Space
Prison Segmentation For Security
Dowsing for Prisoners; Answers from Above
Ex-Prisoner Possibilities With Real Estate Investors
Prison Segmentation For Joint Ventures
Prison Segmentation For Your Rehabilitation: R U Ready?
Prison Segmentation For Family Villages
Prison Segmentation For Senior Prisoners
Prison Segmentation For Coaching Clubs
Prison Segmentation For Miracles
Prison Segmentation For A Prison Game Show
Prison Segmentation For Spousal Support
Prison Segmentation For Exit Contracts
Prison Segmentation For Sentence Segments
Penitentiary Edition Angel Raphael Speaks

Little Books on Kindle.com by Rev. Mike:
English Medical History Questionnaire For Non-English Speakers
English Language Helper For Non-English Speakers
Wise Wonderful Women Are The Well Of The Family
Answers to Test & Research: Dowsing Power
Crisis? Reiki! Baby? Reiki!
Bible References For Healing
Angel Raphael Speaks – Prisons
Angel Raphael Speaks – Veterans
The Saint Off Interstate 95

20 - Angels Please Prayers

Addict's

Angels of Healing Selected
Help Me to Stay Directed
Come To Me From The Sky
I Am Ready to Succeed Not Try
If I Don't Invite You In
I Might Not Win
I Have Been Lost For Too Long
Help Me To Stay Strong

&

Alcoholic's

Angels of Healing On High
Help Me to Stay Dry
Come To Me From The Sky
I Am Ready to Succeed Not Try
If I Don't Invite You In
I Might Not Win
I Have Been Lost For Too Long
Help Me To Stay Strong

From

http://AngelRaphaelSpeaks.com/AAAAAAA/

21 - Private Channeling

Angel Raphael Speaks a series of free messages that are channeled through Reverend Mike Wanner for the Highest good and Highest Healing of all concerned.

Many questions arise about Reverend Mike doing private channeling, and he does help with that so e-mail him.

Reverend Mike is available worldwide as a psychic channel, emotional release facilitator, spiritual energy practitioner & teacher, and public speaker. He looks forward to meeting you soon!

Email - mikewann@voicenet.com 215-342-1270

PRIVATE SPIRITUAL READINGS/channelings or Spiritual Healing Sessions: Telephone or in person.

Rev. Mike is available for individual, intuitive one-on-one sessions with you, his Guide Family, and your Guides. He helps by offering clarity on emotional situations about your life, your purpose, your spirituality, and the release of stuffed emotions and cellular memory.

Connect to the love of your Guides today!

Contact Rev. Mike for an appointment.

Sessions available:

Spiritual Readings
Angel Channeling
Distant Reiki Healing
Distant Clearing of Stuffed Emotions
Distant Clearing Cellular Memory
Distant Clearing Energy Blockages
Distant Clearing of the Chakras
Customized needs
Mastermind dowsing responses to yes/no direction finding questions.

Rev. Mike is a facilitator of healing. He brings you and the Divine together so that you can align with the Divine and have a great time and a great life. All healing is between you and God, as it should be.

Go ahead and start without Rev. Mike. Visit his prayer site http://www.Create-A-Prayer.com. Take the first step NOW.

22 - Reverend Mike Wanner

Rev. Mike Wanner started his spiritual and ministerial studies with Reiki in 1993 and had studied seven styles of Reiki in the U.S., Japan, Canada, Denmark and Australia. He is certified to teach. He became certified to teach Integrated Energy Therapy in 1999 and co-taught the first IET class of the new Millennium. Mike began dowsing in 2001.

Ordained as a Metaphysical Minister of the International Metaphysical Ministry and an Interfaith Minister of the Circle of Miracles Ministry, Rev. Mike practices and teaches spiritual energy therapies in the Philadelphia Area.

Rev. Mike holds ministerial degrees from the University of Metaphysics and the University of Sedona. He is a Pastoral Care Associate at Jefferson - Aria - Frankford Hospital. He taught at the National Academy of Massage Therapy and Health Sciences.

Rev. Mike was a faculty member of the Medical Mission Sister's Center for Human Integration's School of Integrated Body/Mind Therapies in Fox Chase, Philadelphia, PA for twelve years.

Rev. Mike is licensed by the teaching of Intuitional Metaphysics to practice Spiritual Healing and Scientific Prayer. Mike is also a Prayer therapist.

Rev. Mike was elected in 2007 to the status of "Fellow of the American Institute of Stress."

In 2008, Rev. Mike became a practitioner of Coincidental Recognition as he incorporated the CoRe system into his spiritual healing practice.

In 2009, Rev. Mike trademarked a new healing process called Quantum Quatro! Subtle Energy System Support®.
In 2011, Rev. Mike joined the outreach program known as the Health Advantage Group.

In 2012, Rev. Mike became a Certified Professional Coach by The Master Coaching Academy and Joined The Personal Empowerment Group.

Prior to his spiritual, ministerial and coaching studies, Rev. Mike worked for Sears Roebuck and Co. while in High School and after graduation, until he joined the U. S. Air Force in 1965. He returned to Sears from Vietnam in 1969 and stayed until 1978. His final Sears assignment was as an efficiency expert in Methods - Operational Research and Development.

He volunteered with Burholme Emergency Medical Services from 1969 and is still a Life Member and Board of Directors Member. He started a private ambulance company in 1975 and worked professionally in the field until 2001 when he devoted his full attention to real estate investing, healing, coaching, and writing.

www.ReverendMikeWanner.com

www.ingramcontent.com/pod-product-compliance
Lightning Source LLC
Chambersburg PA
CBHW071201220526
45468CB00003B/1113